HELPING CHILDREN THROUGH TRAUMA

HELPING CHILDREN THROUGH TRAUMA

NATISHA DAVIS-WILSON,
PhD, LPC

Copyright © 2023 Natisha Davis-Wilson, PhD, LPC.

All rights reserved. No part of this book may be reproduced, stored, or transmitted by any means—whether auditory, graphic, mechanical, or electronic—without written permission of both publisher and author, except in the case of brief excerpts used in critical articles and reviews. Unauthorized reproduction of any part of this work is illegal and is punishable by law.

ISBN: 979-8-88640-640-5 (sc)
ISBN: 979-8-88640-641-2 (hc)
ISBN: 979-8-88640-642-9 (e)

Because of the dynamic nature of the Internet, any web addresses or links contained in this book may have changed since publication and may no longer be valid. The views expressed in this work are solely those of the author and do not necessarily reflect the views of the publisher, and the publisher hereby disclaims any responsibility for them.

One Galleria Blvd., Suite 1900, Metairie, LA 70001
1-888-421-2397

CONTENTS

Introduction vii

Chapter 1 What is Trauma 1

Chapter 2 Three Types of Traumas 7

Chapter 3 How Trauma Affects Our Children 10

Chapter 4 Developmental Considerations 16

Chapter 5 Untreated Trauma In Children 26

Chapter 6 Helping Children Cope 33

INTRODUCTION

On April 20, 1999, two teens went on a shooting spree killing thirteen people and injuring more than twenty people, before turning the gun on themselves and committing suicide at Columbine High School in Littleton, Colorado. At that time, the Columbine shooting was the worst school shooting in the United States. Seven years later on October 2, 2006, a gunman took hostages and shot ten girls ages ranging between 6–13, killing five, before committing suicide at West Nickel Mines School in Bart Township, Lancaster County, Pennsylvania. In December 2012, a gunman entered Sandy Hook Elementary School and shot and killed twenty-six people. Twenty of the victims were children ranging in age between 6–7 years and six adult staff members. Then we have this latest school shooting in Uvalde, Texas at Robb Elementary. A gunman entered Robb Elementary school and killed nineteen students and two teachers, injuring seventeen others.

The children and adults who die in these school shootings often dominate the news media whereas hundreds of thousands of children's lives have been profoundly impacted. In the Columbine shooting, 1,820 students were at the school when the shooting occurred. Twenty students were present at the West Nickel school when the gunmen went in and took the girls hostage. In the Sandy Hook school shooting, there were 420 kids at school. In addition to the students present at these schools as the shootings occurred, you still have hundreds of thousands of students who suffer no physical wounds at all, but they are haunted by what they saw, heard, or lost.

From tragedies such as these school shootings to the COVID shutdown and war in Ukraine, children are deeply affected. When tragedies occur, it can be difficult for young people to process their emotions and manage their feelings especially when they do not even realize what they are going through.

This book is intended to shed light on children affected by trauma—be it witnessing mass shootings in school, gun violence in the community, physical, emotional, and sexual abuse, to just being in a car accident. No matter how profound the event, traumatized children that go without any form of treatment can easily become the gunmen shooting up the schools, gang leaders, and dysfunctional adults.

CHAPTER 1

WHAT IS TRAUMA

A nine-year-old was sitting in her room playing with her baby dolls when all of a sudden, she hears yelling. She jumps up and runs to see what was going on. The little girl enters her mother's bedroom and began witnessing her mom being beaten up by her mom's boyfriend. For the little girl, this is not the first time she is witnessing this. The little girl has to see this at least once a week. On a few occasions, Mom had to go to the hospital for broken bones, cracked teeth, and black eyes. This child is often left alone while Mom goes to the hospital.

The nine-year-old is an only child and her biological father is not in the picture. This little girl is often absent from school due to her mom's inability to wake up in the mornings. When she does go to school, at times her uniform is unkempt which causes the other children to ridicule her. The little girl suppresses her feelings and keeps to herself. She struggles to maintain any friends and teachers are concerned about her.

The school social worker has attempted to reach out to her mom but she has been uncooperative. The little girl goes into the bathroom at school and cuts herself with a razor she brought from home. Another kid who was in the bathroom thought something was off and went to get help. The teacher came into the bathroom and the little girl began crying uncontrollably.

For this little girl, she has been dealing with a lot of traumas—witnessing her mom being beaten, not having her father in her life, and being ridiculed by the other children at school because her uniform is unkempt. She doesn't feel comfortable talking to the school social worker because she does not want to get her mom into trouble. She loves her mom and her mom has told her not to talk about her business to anyone. However, this little girl can only handle so much before she decides her life is not worth living anymore. Sadly enough, this little girl is not the only child going through trauma.

One may ask, what is trauma? Trauma is an emotional response to a horrifying event. A child's exposure to an incident or series of events that are emotionally disturbing or life-threatening can have long-lasting adverse effects. Children experience trauma differently and what affects one child may not necessarily affect the next child.

For instance, take the above scenario and add a sibling. You have the nine-year-old girl and a thirteen-year-old boy witnessing their mom being beaten, not having a father in their life, and being ridiculed by the other children in school. The nine-year-old may exhibit the same behaviors, whereas, the thirteen-year-old may become more aggressive. He may fight with the other kids at school and even argue back and forth with his mom because he is angry at her for allowing men to hurt her.

So, both kids experienced the same trauma but handled and processed the events of the trauma differently. The nine-year-old holds her pain in and tries to hide what is going on. Meanwhile, the thirteen-year-old is saying "help me" with his aggressive behaviors and arguing back and forth with his mom. It would only take one person to stop and develop a trusting relationship with these kids to get them to open up and share what is going on with themselves.

What are ACEs?

Trauma can happen at any age. When traumatic events happen to children, we call them ACEs (Adverse Childhood Experiences). Adverse Childhood Experiences are traumatic events that occur during childhood (0–17). They have long-lasting negative effects on health, well-being, and opportunity. Not everyone who experiences a stressful event will develop trauma, but everyone will experience some kind of traumatic event at some point in their lifetime, if that makes any sense to you.

Trauma comes in many shapes and forms. Research indicates that children are more vulnerable to trauma but are also more resilient to overcoming trauma if the trauma is treated.

Traumatic events can include:

- Domestic violence

- Gun violence in the community

- Rape and molestation

- Accidents

- Natural disasters

- Physical, sexual, and emotional abuse

- Death of a loved one

- Childhood neglect

- Poverty

- World pandemic

A traumatic event can be anything that causes a lot of stress. Take for instance, a seven-year-old boy attending school. This seven-year-old is in the second grade. Two fourth graders come along and slap this second grader in the face, take his lunch, and eat it. To this seven-year-old boy, he has now experienced a traumatic event. Being bullied can lead to a sense of horror, helplessness, and feeling unsafe to the point where now this boy does not want to go to school anymore.

Another traumatic event can be a child diagnosed with a medical condition. That sense of helplessness and uncertainty of being well again is a traumatic event. Being hospitalized and away from one's home and parents can be very scary to a child.

Traumatic events include things that happen to you directly or someone you are close to, such as a parent, sibling, friend, or relative. Kids take on the stress of others. They sense when something is not right and react. An event can be traumatic for kids whether they witness it for themselves or not.

Wyatt is an eleven-year-old boy who lives in the home with his mom, dad, and older brother. Wyatt's older brother is seventeen years old and hangs out with the wrong crowd. Wyatt observes his brother's behaviors as his brother is a member of a local street gang. Wyatt's brother gets into trouble often at school and in the community. He has been arrested for stealing cars and being in possession of a gun. Wyatt's parents are constantly worried about his brother. They focus a lot of their attention and energy on fixing the brother. Meanwhile, Wyatt is being neglected. Not intentionally, because the parents love and appreciate Wyatt, but the brother has problems that overshadow Wyatt.

Wyatt is internalizing everything that is going on. When he hears sirens or sees the police, he thinks that they are coming for his brother. One day, there was a knock at the door. It was the police coming to tell the family that Wyatt's brother was badly injured in a shootout and was in critical condition at the local hospital. The police explained what happened and the parents and

Wyatt rushed off to go and be with the brother. The brother did recover after months in rehabilitation. He had to learn to walk and talk again. Wyatt did his best to keep it together as his brother and parents went back and forth to doctor's appointments and managed home life. The house was upside down as modifications had to be made to accommodate the brother's medical condition. Wyatt has to now adapt to his family's new circumstances. For Wyatt, this is a traumatic event.

CHAPTER 2

THREE TYPES OF TRAUMAS

Trauma can be divided into three main types: Acute, Chronic, and Complex.

Acute trauma is the result of a single incident or occurrence. The single incident is extreme enough to cause severe emotional or physical distress. The event causes a long-lasting impression on the person's mind. Examples of acute trauma can be:

- a car accident
- a rape
- an assault
- or natural disaster

Michelle is a sixteen-year-old female. She lives at home with her mom and dad. Recently, Michelle and her family were out celebrating her parents' wedding anniversary. They went to a nice dinner and had a wonderful time. Driving home was fun as well as they were reminiscing about the good times they have had as a family. Upon entering their home, they were laughing and in a good mood. Dad noticed that the front door was open and he told Michelle and her mom to step back and let him see what was going on first before they entered the home. Dad and the family realized that the home was burglarized. They called the police and while they were waiting, Michelle cried. She wondered why would anyone do this. She went into her room and noticed her room was ransacked and they had stolen her jewelry and laptop computer.

Michelle has acute trauma from a single incident, where she experienced her home being burglarized. While she may feel different emotions, the event was a single episode and should cause only minimal damage.

Chronic trauma is the result of repeated and prolonged exposure to incidents and occurrences. Children exposed to chronic trauma have a higher risk of mental health problems. Some examples of chronic trauma can be repeated abuse or domestic violence.

Nicole is a seven-year-old female who lives at home with her mom and dad. Nicole's mom is a stay-at-home mom while Nicole's dad is a truck driver. Nicole's dad comes home from being on the road at times and argues and fights with mom. Nicole continues to witness Mom and Dad having domestic altercations. The chronic trauma comes into play because it's the repeated and prolonged exposure of Nicole witnessing her mom and dad's domestic violence.

Complex trauma is the result of experiencing multiple traumatic events, often disturbing and invasive in nature. Complex trauma usually occurs early in life and disrupts the child's development. Complex and chronic trauma are very similar but differ in such that chronic trauma is repeated and prolonged while complex trauma deals with multiple events.

Michael is a ten-year-old boy currently living in foster care. Michael's biological parents are addicted to drugs. Michael's parents were neglectful and his dad was abusive towards Michael. Michael's dad beat him really bad when he was five years old. Michael was in the hospital for broken ribs and fractured skull damage. Michael's mom and dad went to jail for the abuse and lost custody of Michael.

At first, Michael was placed in the home with his maternal grandmother but she became ill and was unable to care for him any longer on a full-time basis. Michael now lives with loving foster parents and still has a relationship with his maternal grandmother. His parents are not allowed to make any kind of contact with him.

Michael has several traumas going on here. He has to deal with the verbal and physical abuse from his mom, and the verbal and physical abuse from his dad. He was hospitalized from his abuse, removed from his home with his parents, removed from the home with his grandmother, living with foster parents, and starting over at a new school.

CHAPTER 3

HOW TRAUMA AFFECTS OUR CHILDREN

Children experience a heightened state of stress during terrible events, and their bodies release hormones related to stress and fear. Trauma can disrupt normal brain development.

As a result, trauma, especially ongoing trauma, can significantly affect a child's long-term emotional development, mental health, physical health, and behavior.

Trauma can have a significant impact on a child's ability to cope and function. It affects a person's body as well as the mind, making the person more susceptible to physical health problems. There are some common symptoms of trauma that may be expected following an occurrence. These symptoms are considered normal and can go away if treated properly. Here is a list of common symptoms:

- Intrusive thoughts of the event that may occur out of the blue or when reminded of the event

- Nightmares

- Visual images of the event

- Hypervigilance - feeling more guarded and being more aware of your surroundings

- Temporary loss of memory where the brain is blocking out some of the events that occurred to protect the person, but the memory does eventually return

- Hyperarousal - feeling more on edge. This is part of your body's natural protection system.

- Fear and anxiety

- Feeling unsafe especially in situations or places that remind you of your traumatic event

- Mood swings

Let's go back to acute trauma and take the incidence of Michelle and the break-in. For a while, (1–3 months) Michelle has to adjust to what happened to her and her family. Their home was broken into and she may feel violated. Michelle now has nightmares where she is dreaming that she was there and witnessed what happened. Her mind keeps playing visual images of her seeing her room or seeing the front door open. As she walks home from school, she looks around, making sure no one is following her, and wonders if anyone of the people hanging around the house could have been the ones who broke in. The family had an alarm company come out and install a new alarm system. They walked her step by step on how to utilize the new system.

Michelle learned the codes to the door and can see the video cameras. Michelle slowly starts to return to her safe place as two and three months pass by. She feels safe now being in her home with her parents and doesn't feel like anyone is going to break in again.

The following symptoms presented can be an indication that a person may be at risk for developing Post-traumatic Stress Disorder. Therefore, it is very important to be aware of the following symptoms:

- Recurrent, involuntary intrusive thoughts that will not go away

- Loss of interest in activities that you used to once enjoy, as well as feelings of being detached from others

- Isolation from others, including important sources of social support

- Avoidance - it is very common to avoid certain situations, activities, or people after the traumatic event. However, you must pay attention to avoidance behaviors. Avoidance usually leads to more avoidance as it reinforces the belief that the world is not a safe place. This avoidance can then lead to a worsening of symptoms and eventually PTSD, or even depression or severe anxiety.

- Unhealthy coping behaviors - use of alcohol, drugs, sex, shopping, etc., as a way to avoid thoughts and feelings

Now let's go back to chronic and complex trauma. Chronic and complex trauma can definitely cause a child to present with PTSD risk symptoms. Let's review Michael, he had complex trauma. He had multiple traumas he had to deal with. Michael exhibits symptoms of detachment. He lost his relationship with his parents, and his relationship with his grandmother changed as he was removed from her home. He doesn't feel safe emotionally in his new environment with his foster parents. He stays to himself at school because he doesn't want anyone to know his situation. Michael feels uncomfortable talking in class, he has no friends, and he doesn't participate in any extracurricular activities. Michael avoids anyone and everything. He does draw very well and creates anime characters which he keeps to himself.

Now let's go back to Nicole, remember I said she held everything in. She suppresses her feelings of fear and anxiety every time her parents would fight. If Nicole was older, she might turn to alcohol and drugs to escape from her parents' fighting. At her age now, she may use food as comfort eating to the point where it makes her sick all the time. She is constantly coming home from school early because she does not feel well. She is aggressive and fights with other kids in her class. Nicole is sad all the time and has crying spells. Nicole is also detached from her parents. She stays in her room, out of sight. When it's just Nicole and her mom at home, she may spend time with her mom but superficially. She doesn't talk or share about any true emotions she may be experiencing. To her mom, she will present like everything is okay.

Another consideration to take into account would be the cause and effect that trauma has. Trauma events that children may experience can set into motion a domino effect in their lives. It's called cause and effect. Because this happened, now this must happen. Changes in the child's life can be challenging and very difficult for the child to adjust to. Effects can be things such as changes in their living environment, where they attend school, who they are living with, and if they are now living with an injury or disability. Changes in one's daily routines can be challenging under normal circumstances but it is exacerbated after a traumatic event occurs. Other factors to take into consideration are:

- Will there be ongoing criminal or civil proceedings

- Reminders such as people, places, or things of the trauma event

- Anniversary of the trauma

Some children who go through trauma don't exhibit symptoms of trauma. Different factors come into play when a child experiences trauma such as:

- Has this child experienced trauma before?

- Severity of the event - How bad was the trauma? Was anyone hurt or injured? Did anyone die? Were the police involved?

- Witness or hearsay - Was the child present when the trauma occurred or did they hear about what happened?

- Other people's reaction - How did everyone around the child respond? Were people calm or panicking? Was there crying, screaming, or yelling?

- Culture reactions

CHAPTER 4

DEVELOPMENTAL CONSIDERATIONS

Now you have a family of three children and a mother. The father had terminal cancer and has recently passed away. The oldest child is a seventeen-year-old boy. The middle child is an eleven-year-old female and the baby is literally a baby, a one-year-old boy. Now in this scenario, Mom has to grieve the loss of her husband, whom she has been married to for over twenty years. She also has to help her kids grieve the loss of their father. Four people, three children, four different developmental stages, four different temperaments.

What children understand during and after an exposure to a traumatic event is a function of their developmental level with respect to cognitive, emotional, and social factors. Taking all the developmental theories into consideration, a listed summary is below to describe how children respond to trauma.

Understanding the impact that traumatic events cause at any age can help to identify areas of personal development that may need to be addressed. The body's biology develops throughout infancy and adolescence. A child's development can be defined as the process by which a child changes and processes things over time. Depending on who you are referencing from Jean Piaget to Erik Erikson, to even Sigmund Freud, they all classify stages of development in groups by age categories. Normal developmental functioning is partly determined by the environment in which the child grows up. However, some stay stuck at a certain stage due to trauma while others can go on and be developmentally stage- and age-appropriate. When a child experiences trauma, the immune system and the body's stress response systems may not develop normally.

Infancy: birth – 18 months

Erik Erikson believed that during this time the infant struggles with trust versus mistrust. It's during this stage of development that the infant is learning to feed. They are helpless and depend on their parents or caregivers for their emotional needs. If the infant cries, they want to know that they will be fed, changed, and nurtured in all aspects. Success in this stage leads to the infant having a sense of trust when his/her needs are met.

When babies are exposed to life-threatening or traumatic events at this stage of development, they may experience:

- High levels of distress such as frequent crying

- Loss of emotional reactions such as laughing, cooing

- Not meeting milestones of walking, talking, or even feeding

Going back to the scenario at the beginning of this chapter, let's take the one-year-old baby boy and use him for this example. Let's call baby boy Leroy. Now Leroy's dad just died of terminal cancer. The family around him is grieving. Leroy was a happy baby before the death of his dad. He met his developmental milestones of walking, feeding himself, and saying some words. He experiences this trauma and now all of a sudden, he is constantly crying all the time. His laughter is gone and he keeps a stone-cold shocked or numb look on his face. He no longer eats by himself and wants to be held and fed. This lasts until he can feel secure again. He also starts thumb-sucking as a reflex of comforting himself. He can come out of this with Mom being of comfort to him and also his siblings showing love and comfort to him, assuring him that everything will be alright.

Early Childhood: 2 - 3 years old

Erik Erikson believed that during this time in early childhood, two- to three-year-olds are struggling with autonomy versus shame and doubt. It's during this stage that they develop a sense of personal control over physical skills and also develop a sense of independence. They should be mastering toilet training, and their language skills should be getting stronger as they are utilizing new words. Their social skills are developing and they are showing more emotions. Many people believe that babies cannot experience trauma or they think that babies do not notice when things are off. This is totally untrue. Babies are used to routine; they sense when things are off or notice when their caregiver is no longer around. As traumatic events occur in early childhood, these children do feel it and they react. When two- to three-year-olds experience trauma at this stage of development, they may experience:

- High levels of distress such as frequent crying

- Loss of emotional reactions such as playfulness, friendliness towards other people, making friends

- Thumb-sucking

- Delayed toilet training

- Stuttering

During the early months and up to three years of age, babies are very sensitive to problems affecting their parents and/or caretakers. This can include if the caretaker is sad, scared, or in any kind of distress. They sense changes in the household such as noise levels. Babies feel when adults are raising their voices in arguments, that is why you see babies start to cry or scream when two people are arguing. Just remember, when a parent or caretaker is affected by something, so are the babies.

Preschool: 3 – 5 years old

Erik Erikson believed that during this time in the preschool years, three- to five-year-olds are struggling with initiative versus guilt. They are exploring their sense of purpose. They are beginning to assert control and power over the environment. Preschoolers are very vulnerable to traumatic events. Their language is still developing and they cannot express what they are feeling or going through. They do not have the words to communicate and it comes out in their behaviors. Preschoolers may not know exactly what is going on but they can still sense that something is not right. Some behaviors that preschoolers may exhibit are:

- Being clingy to the parent or caretakers

- Sleeping issues - fear of the dark, bad dreams, scared to go to sleep

- Bed-wetting

- Becoming aggressive towards other children

- Being fearful/jumpy/withdrawn

- Feeling sick with complaints about headaches or stomach aches

Trauma can slow things down or get in the way of preschoolers learning new things. They can start to regress or develop long-lasting behavior problems. Preschoolers' brains may not fully comprehend what is going on. They tend to blame themselves and lose their sense of feeling safe. It is up to the parent and caretaker to help this preschooler feel safe again. Preschool-aged children (ages 3–5) are most likely to express their concerns about safety in terms of separation from parents and other primary caretakers. They rely on cues from caretakers about danger. They don't have the cognition yet to fully understand the finality of death. They may feel something being not right and may exhibit some regressive behaviors, such as bed-wetting, thumb-sucking, or fear of the dark. They may also have symptoms of fear, anxiety, sleep problems, and aggressive behaviors.

Let's use Rondell as an example. Rondell is a five-year-old boy who just experienced being bitten by a dog. He was playing football on his front lawn and an aggressive pit bull belonging to a man in the neighborhood is out unleashed. The dog comes running straight to Rondell and bites him in the face as Rondell fell to the ground running from the dog. Rondell is screaming and hollering and his dad comes running out of the house to save him from the dog. Rondell's dad kicks and throws things at the dog to get the dog away. The owner finally comes and gets the dog.

Rondell has to go to the hospital to get stitches and tetanus shots and continues to be in pain for days. This was a very traumatic incident for him. For weeks now, Rondell has been sleeping in the bed with his parents, he has a fear of going outside to play, and he started wetting the bed and talking baby talk. Rondell's parents have been very supportive of him since he was bitten by the dog. His parents attempt to calm him down by holding him and cuddling with him in the bed. They let Rondell know that he is safe from the harm of the dog. The dog has been taken to animal control and is not allowed to be back with the owner.

School-Aged Children: 6 – 11

Erik Erikson believed that school-aged children go through the basic conflict of industry versus inferiority. They are in school now and have a sense of competence. They are developing coping skills to deal with social and academic demands. School-aged children are more vocal and can express their thoughts and feelings better. They know what hurts, what's going on around them, and can see things going on in their parents' lives. They are able to read facial gestures and look for context clues. With this in mind, school-aged children are able to handle difficulties as they arise but they still look to and need the adults around them to comfort and guide them. Some behaviors that school-aged children may exhibit after a trauma can include:

- Withdrawal from social situations

- Isolation from family and friends

- Denial that the trauma even occurred

- Suppressing their feelings and pretending to be okay when they are not

- Anxiety

- Mood swings and crying spells

- Anger (easily frustrated)

- Sleep issues

- Blaming themselves

- Somatic symptoms (complaining about illness such as headaches and stomach aches, consistently)

- School academic problems (failing classes, incomplete work, behavior problems in school)

Elementary school-aged children (6 – 11 years) are prone to polarizing situations into "right" and "wrong." They get their sense of security from clear-cut rules. As they mature from six to twelve years of age, they begin to develop an increasing sense of empathy and altruism. When exposed to trauma, children in this age group may fear for others and recognize death as final. These kids are profoundly affected by exposure to a traumatic event, even if they are not involved directly. They may exhibit symptoms of school avoidance, somatic complaints (e.g., headaches, stomachaches), irrational fears, sleep problems, nightmares, irritability, and angry outbursts. They may also exhibit some attention problems and struggle with their schoolwork.

Adolescence: 12 – 18

Erik Erikson believed that adolescents struggle with identity versus role confusion. They are experiencing social relationships and getting a sense of self and personal identity. Adolescents are trying to develop the ability to stay true to themselves but what happens when they experience trauma? They are already going through trying times. Adolescents have so many changes going on within their body and brain development. They are struggling with independence from their parents and have the mentality that it won't happen to me.

Adolescents have cognitive awareness of the trauma going on. They understand the finality of death and are vulnerable to the notion of what could I have done to prevent this event. Traumatic events can make them feel out of control. Adolescent responses to trauma are more similar to adult responses. They include:

- Intrusive thoughts
- Hypervigilance
- Emotional numbing
- Nightmares and sleep disturbances
- Avoidance
- They are at increased risk of having problems with substance abuse, peer problems, and depression.

Trauma is often associated with intense feelings of humiliation, self-blame, shame, and guilt, which result from the sense of powerlessness and may lead to a sense of alienation and avoidance.

Now in the scenario at the beginning of this chapter, Mom and the oldest child would be on the same developmental level. Mom and the oldest child are aware that Dad has died and is not coming back. They understand that he died from a terminal illness, however, the adolescent may wonder, could I have done anything differently? If I would have kept my room clean, or stayed out of trouble, could that have made Dad worry less, stress less, and therefore he could have lived longer? This adolescent may not express the feelings that he has and rather, have nightmares, avoid being around others, and even utilize drugs and alcohol.

For the eleven-year-old, she understands that Dad is dead and not coming back. She is more worried about Mom and her older brother and wants them to be okay. The eleven-year-old starts to exhibit somatic symptoms. Her stomach and her head hurt. She goes to school but has to call Mom to come and pick her up because she feels sick. She is not sleeping and her grades are falling behind.

Now let's take baby Leroy and make him three years old. Baby Leroy does not realize that Dad is gone forever. He gets his cues from Mom and his siblings. He continues to feel secure because his needs are still being taken care of by Mom. He knows that Dad is not there anymore and will forget that Dad was ever there and will only remember what is told to him by his family from here on out.

CHAPTER 5

UNTREATED TRAUMA IN CHILDREN

Kaicy is a twenty-two-year-old female who experienced trauma when she was seven years old. At the age of seven, Kaicy was in the grocery store with her mom getting food to cook for dinner.

The grocery store was not a big chain grocery as it was in a small community. Everyone pretty much knew one another in the community and looked out for one another. The community did have some problems with a certain group of teenagers. On this particular day when Kaicy and her mom were in the grocery, the teenagers came in to rob the store. When one of the cashiers hesitated, one of the teenagers shot the cashier right in front of Kaicy and her mom. Blood actually splattered on Kaicy's clothes and shoes. Kaicy was severely impacted by this traumatic event.

Kaicy became anxious and fearful of everything. She had bad dreams when she went to sleep at night. Kaicy even wet the bed. She had a hard time concentrating in school and her grades fell behind. Mom excused Kaicy's grades as she knew it was from the trauma. Mom did not seek help for herself or for Kaicy. As Kaicy got older, she started cutting herself when she felt overwhelmed. She missed a lot of school as she was not understanding her work and hung out with the wrong crowd. Kaicy dropped out of school and started doing drugs. Her mom became unable to accept Kaicy's behaviors so she put her out and Kaicy became homeless by the time she was eighteen years old. Kaicy lived on the streets for about a year before she finally got help.

The impact of untreated trauma in children can negatively affect a child's development. Children may develop unhealthy ways of coping that allow them to survive and function from day to day. During the traumatic experience, the child's brain is in a heightened state of stress. Fear-related hormones are then activated letting the brain know that something is wrong. Although, stress is a normal part of life, when a child is exposed to chronic trauma, like abuse or neglect, the child's brain remains in this heightened pattern. Remaining in this heightened state can change the emotional, behavioral, and cognitive functioning of the child in order to maintain and promote survival. Over time, these traumatic experiences can have a significant impact on a child's future behavior, emotional development, and mental and physical health.

As we take a look at Kaicy and her experience, we see her experienced trauma which was witnessing the cashier get shot. We see that she received no mental health treatment and it caused her to go into survival mode. It took her from the age of seven to twenty to get help. Kaicy went on a downward spiral.

Some kids can move on from traumatic events with no problems while other kids need a helping hand. Without proper treatment and repeated childhood exposure to trauma, kids are at a high risk of unhealthy risky behaviors such as smoking, eating disorders, and substance use. It can also lead to the increased use of health and mental health services by being in and out of treatment for periods of time. Some kids end up in the child welfare system or juvenile justice systems. Adult survivors of trauma may have difficulty establishing fulfilling relationships, maintaining employment, and even taking care of their own kids. Post-traumatic Stress Disorder, Depression, and Anxiety Disorders are common mental health diagnoses that are derived from trauma in kids. Some kids get misdiagnosed with Attention Deficit Hyperactivity Disorder, Oppositional Defiant Disorder, and even Conduct Disorder when it's actual trauma causing the behaviors. Trauma can mimic these disorders such as:

- Being inattentive or being distracted/not focused can look like attention deficit hyperactivity disorder

- Aggression can cause some defiance and look like oppositional defiant disorder

- Aggression and defiance from the trauma can cause conduct-related actions giving the child a diagnosis of conduct disorder

Post-traumatic Stress Disorder (PTSD) - is a mental health disorder that is triggered by a traumatic experience or event that a person has either experienced or witnessed. After a traumatic experience, a person may temporarily go through periods where they struggle with symptoms of the trauma but after some time, they are able to return back to their regular functioning. PTSD becomes diagnosed when the person experiences symptoms of trauma lasting longer than four months, that interfere with home/work/school functioning.

Symptoms of PTSD consist of:

- intrusive thoughts
- not being able to sleep
- recurrent nightmares
- feeling anxious
- feeling overwhelmed
- avoiding thinking about the trauma and people associated with the trauma
- negative changes in their mood.

Anxiety is very prevalent among children and adults. Nearly 20 percent of adults have been diagnosed with an anxiety disorder, such as panic disorder, generalized anxiety disorder, phobias, and social anxiety. Symptoms of anxiety disorders frequently overlap.

Generalized Anxiety Disorder (GAD) - is a mental health disorder that can also be triggered by a traumatic experience or event that a person has either experienced or witnessed. It's pretty normal to get stressed out and worry about things going on around you. It's even normal to feel overwhelmed with life at times. GAD gets diagnosed in a person who has gone through trauma when the trauma symptoms are long-lasting and affects daily functioning at work, school, and in social settings. Because post-traumatic stress disorder and anxiety share similar symptoms, it can be hard to distinguish between the two disorders. These are some signs and symptoms that they share:

- Extreme worry

- Insomnia or restlessness

- Irritability and other changes in mood or thinking

- Difficulty concentrating

- Sweating

- Hypervigilance

- Avoidance of people, places, or things

- Symptoms cause significant impairment or distress in a person's life

PTSD can co-occur with generalized anxiety disorder (GAD). However, the major difference between GAD and PTSD is the root cause of the disorder. PTSD develops in response to a traumatic experience that is witnessed or through direct exposure of the trauma. In GAD, trauma may exacerbate symptoms of GAD, or vice versa. GAD may also impact how an individual responds to a traumatic event and causes excessive worrying.

Depression - There is a large consensus indicating that childhood trauma is significantly involved in the development of depression and even leaves people at a higher risk for suicide. Traumatic experiences in childhood can be found in most psychosocial assessments given to children, adolescents, and adults as they seek help for symptoms of depression. The results of these assessments find that childhood trauma can dramatically increase the risk of a person to be diagnosed with Major Depressive Disorder.

Depression goes beyond feeling temporarily sad or anxious to lasting longer than six months. A kid who is depressed might be feeling:

- Overwhelmed

- Tired

- Hopeless

- Have loss of interest or pleasure in doing things

- Feeling down or sad

- Poor appetite

- Feel bad about themselves

- Have trouble concentrating

- Thoughts that they may be better off dead or hurting themselves in some kind of way

- They might also be unfairly blaming themselves for their circumstances and the way they feel.

CHAPTER 6

HELPING CHILDREN COPE

After a traumatic event, it is the body's normal response to experience a range of emotions. Your comfort, support, and reassurance can make the child feel safe, help them manage their fears, and guide them through a healthy recovery. Helping children cope with trauma immediately following the traumatic event can make a big difference in a child's life moving forward. Getting help can prevent symptoms of trauma from becoming severe and thus help the child to have a speedy recovery.

There are important roles that everyone in the child's support system can play which includes the parents/caregivers, teachers, and mental health professionals.

Parents/Caretakers: Parenting a child who has experienced trauma can be difficult. You may feel like no one understands what you are going through and may even struggle with past trauma yourself. However, there are strategies that you can utilize to help you help your child.

- Begin by making every effort to provide a safe recovery environment. A traumatized child can benefit from your touch, extra cuddling, hugs, or just a reassuring pat on the back. It gives them a feeling of security, which is so important in the aftermath of a frightening or disturbing event.

- Reduce ongoing exposure to stressors/secondary traumas. Change people, places, and things that may cause continued harm to the child.

- Reestablish normal roles and routines. Routines reassure children that life will be okay again. As much as you can, try to have a regular mealtime and bedtime.

- Activate support among kinship networks and spiritual and community systems.

- Encourage the child to do fun activities and engage in playing with other peers.

- Talk about what happened with the child. Answer their questions to the best of your ability. It's always best that they learn what happened from you as the trusted adult. Be brief and honest.

- Prevent/limit exposure to news coverage as you don't want to over-expose them or re-traumatize them again and again.

- Acknowledge what your child is feeling and let them know it is okay for them to have their feelings.

So, let's go back to the case of Wyatt. Wyatt and his family experienced the trauma of the brother being in trouble and getting shot. The family's life was upside down. Here is how the parents can help Wyatt with his trauma. Wyatt internalizes everything going on. Mom and Dad can talk to Wyatt and express their love and support for him. They can lay down rules for the brother moving forward to secure their safety. The parents can keep Wyatt involved in his normal activities and routine schedule. For example, if Wyatt played baseball, make sure he goes to practice and his games as scheduled. Dad can spend some one-on-one time with Wyatt so they can talk about what happened and establish some bonding moments. Both parents can make sure to acknowledge what Wyatt is feeling and that it is okay for him to feel this way.

It is important that the parents/caretakers observe any changes in the child's behavior such as their appetite, energy level, sleep patterns, and academic performance after they experience a traumatic event. Reaching out to the child and making sure they feel secure and comfortable in opening up to you is very essential.

Take Care of Yourself:

- It's also important to take care of yourself and your own emotional well-being while on the journey of treating your child.

- Know when to ask for additional help from the school and a mental health professional.

School: As a teacher, it can be somewhat difficult to focus your attention on one student when you have a classroom of over thirty students. You may see a child acting out or being disruptive and think they have behavior problems and send them out of the classroom so that you can get back to teaching. However, if you know that a kid has been through a traumatic event, there are strategies that you can utilize to help you be able to help that child.

- Re-establish roles and routines as much as possible. Children function better when they know what to expect. Returning to a school routine will help students feel that the troubling events have not taken control over every aspect of their daily lives.

- Assess needs that may warrant intervention and be aware of signs that the child may need extra help. Students who are unable to function due to feelings of intense sadness, distress, fear, or anger should be referred to a mental health professional. Watch out for the child complaining of headaches, stomachaches, or extreme fatigue.

- Consider a school memorial. School memorials should be kept brief and appropriate to the needs and age range of the general school community.

- Communicate with the child letting them know you are there for them. You can reassure the child/children that school officials are making sure they are safe. They may feel comforted when they know that trusted adults are doing what they can to take care of them.

- Stay in communication with parents. Let them know about the school's programs and activities so they can be prepared for discussions that may continue at home.

- Take care of yourself. You may be so busy helping your students that you neglect yourself. Find ways to give yourself self-care.

Now let's go back to the very beginning with the nine-year-old. Let's call the nine-year-old Lauren. Lauren broke down at school. She told her teacher everything that has been going on with her. Lauren tells the teacher she witnessed her mom being beaten up by her boyfriend and how the kids at the school tease her and call her names. The teacher can comfort Lauren by offering words of encouragement. She can reach out to the mom and offer support to the mom. The teacher can also get with the school and give

Lauren a uniform voucher to help with her unkempt uniforms. The teacher can also talk with the other students about bullying and teasing in an attempt to protect her from ongoing trauma.

Mental Health Professionals: Helping children cope with trauma may also involve intensive outpatient psychotherapy, medication, self-care, or a combination of these approaches. Treatments for trauma often focus on helping children to be able to integrate their emotional response to the trauma as well as addressing any resulting mental health conditions such as anxiety, depression, or PTSD.

- Provide a safe environment for the child and the family to be able to come in and work through their trauma.

- Assess needs that may warrant intervention, such as severe or persistent distress, numbing, or impairment; reduced capacity of family/community to support the child; self-destructive or violent behaviors.

- Identify trauma-exposed children and provide culturally appropriate information and support.

- Help children and families make connections for follow-up and intervention.

- Make sure the therapy is developmentally appropriate for the child.

- Provide anxiety management.

- Provide relaxation strategies.

- Provide Trauma-Focused Cognitive Behavioral Therapy.

- Provide consultation to professionals in schools, health care settings, spiritual settings, and other service systems who see trauma-exposed children and families.

- If you treat children, obtain training in developmentally and culturally appropriate evidence-based therapies for child trauma to effectively treat children who do not recover on their own.

- Help the child and family understand expected/normal trauma reactions, identify and use their existing coping skills, and know when to ask for additional help.

www.ingramcontent.com/pod-product-compliance
Lightning Source LLC
LaVergne TN
LVHW092335081225
827336LV00034B/542